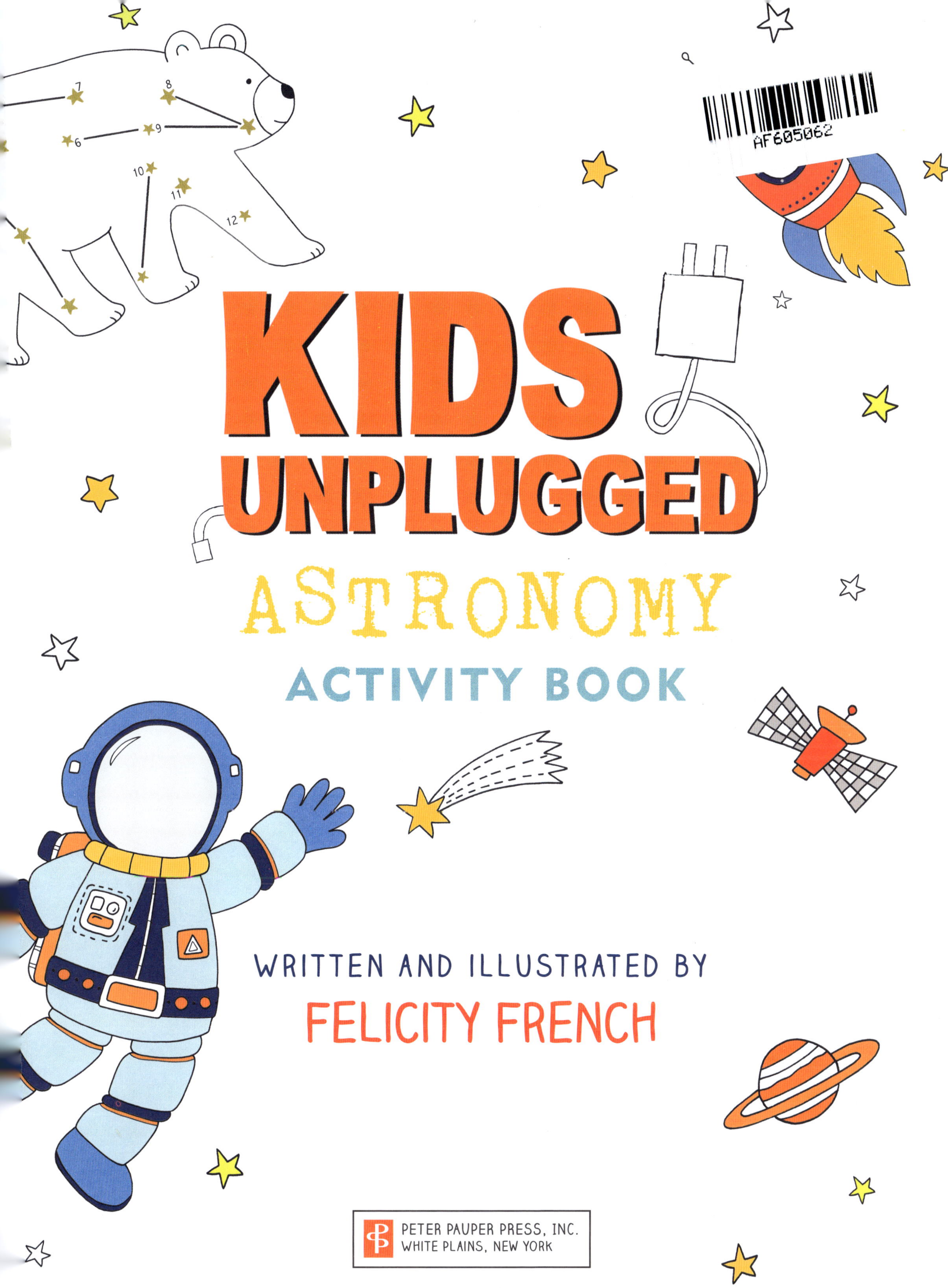

KIDS UNPLUGGED

ASTRONOMY ACTIVITY BOOK

WRITTEN AND ILLUSTRATED BY
FELICITY FRENCH

PETER PAUPER PRESS, INC.
WHITE PLAINS, NEW YORK

Manufactured for Peter Pauper Press, Inc.
202 Mamaroneck Avenue
White Plains, NY 10601 USA

ISBN 978-1-4413-2420-7

Printed in China

Published in the United Kingdom and Europe by
Peter Pauper Press, Inc. c/o White Pebble International
Unit 2, Plot 11 Terminus Road
Chichester, West Sussex PO19 8TX, UK

7 6 5 4 3 2

Visit us at www.peterpauper.com

3...2...1... blast off!

Have you ever looked up at the night sky and admired the stars? So have a lot of other people for countless years! A person who studies the stars is called an astronomer, and the science of studying space (say that three times fast!) is called astronomy. Since the dawn of astronomy, so many interesting facts about our universe have been uncovered. For example, did you know that the biggest hurricanes on Jupiter and Neptune are so huge they could fit multiple Earths inside them? And did you know that Mars at one time might have had oceans just like Earth's?

Within this book, you'll find tons of out-of-this-world facts as well as a galaxy of puzzles and activities that'll be sure to send your brain into orbit! So strap in and get ready for lift off into a universe of space adventure—no passwords required!

ANSWERS ARE IN THE BACK OF THE BOOK.

BIG BANG

The birth of the universe started with the Big Bang over 13.7 billion years ago! It took over 9 billion years before Earth and other planets were formed, and over 10 billion years before the first life on Earth arose!

3 seconds later, high-energy reactions occur, creating the first particles (or building blocks for everything in the universe)

300,000 years later the first atoms form

A few hundred million years later the first galaxies and stars form

Mercury
Venus
Earth
Mars
Jupiter
Saturn
Uranus
Neptune
Draw in the sun at the top of this map and color in our solar system!
9 billion years later the solar system forms, including Earth
Color in these signs of life!
10 billion years later the first life on Earth begins

SOLAR SCRAMBLE

A group of objects (planets, comets, asteroids, and more) that move around a star is called a solar system. Our solar system contains eight planets and one star, plus countless smaller objects! Unscramble the letters below to discover the biggest objects in our solar system!

DID YOU KNOW?

Except for Earth, all of the planets in our solar system are named after Roman gods and goddesses. For example, the second planet from the sun, Venus, was named after the Roman goddess of love and beauty!

Why not draw some comets in too?

The path a planet takes around a star is called an orbit. On a map, these orbits are represented by rings around a star. Design your own solar system map by adding more planets into the orbits below. What would you call the planets in your solar system?

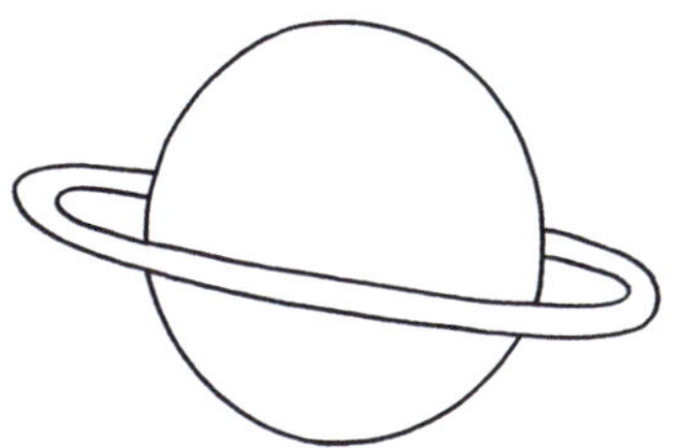

Don't forget to color your map when you're finished.

The Moon

In 1610, astronomer Galileo Galilei pointed a telescope toward the moon. Back then, most people thought the moon was perfectly smooth. But thanks to the telescope, Galileo discovered that wasn't true at all! Instead, Galileo discovered that the moon is covered with craters and mountains!

Draw yourself looking through the telescope!

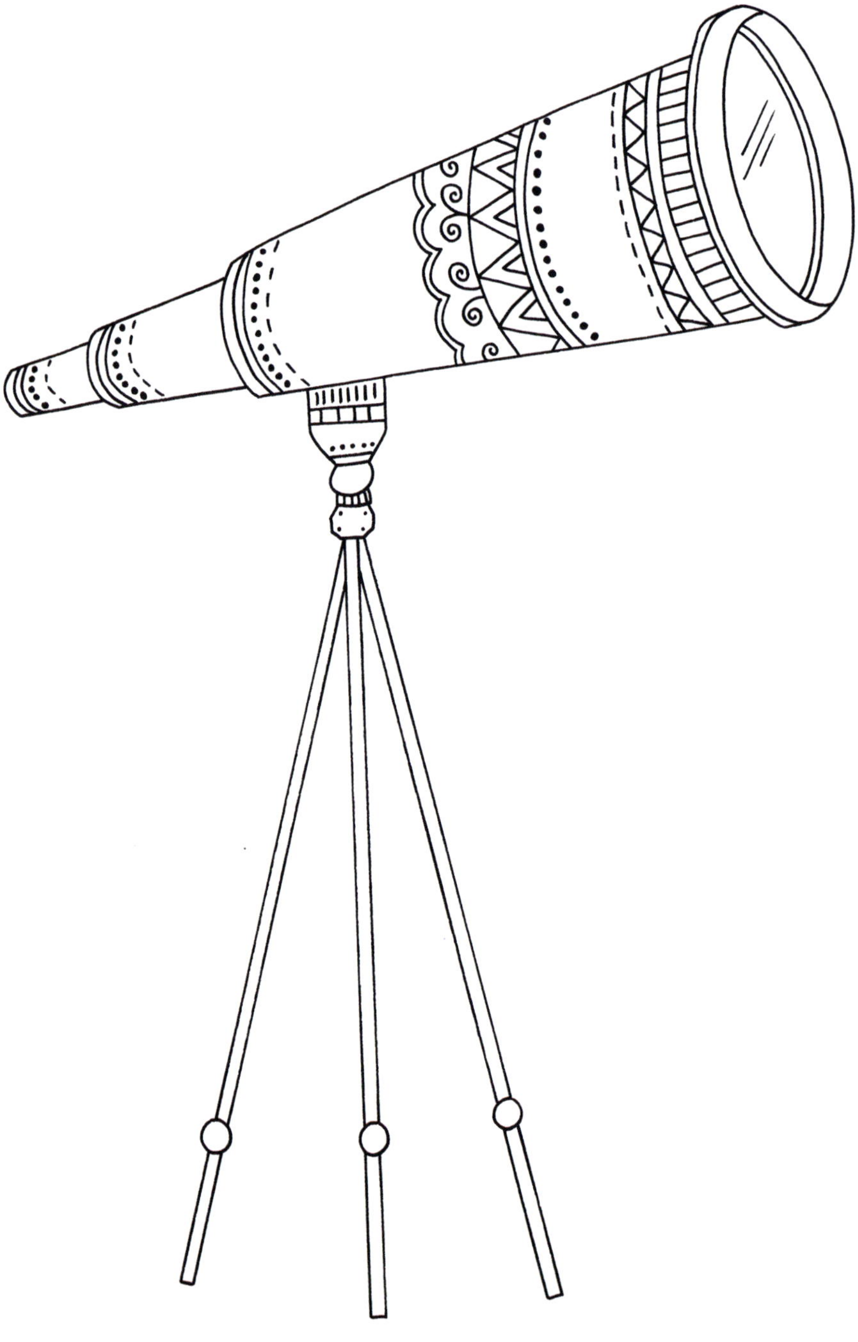

Finish drawing craters and mountains on the moon and fill the sky with stars!

DID YOU KNOW?

Moons are also called **NATURAL SATELLITES**. (Not to be confused with artificial satellites, which are machines we put into orbit around the Earth to help us communicate or study the universe.) Our planet's only moon is not the biggest satellite in the solar system, but it's one of the top five!

Starting on the first day of the month, track the phases of the moon by drawing how it looks every night!

Day 1	Day 2	Day 3	Day 4	Day 5	Day 6
Day 7	Day 8	Day 9	Day 10	Day 11	Day 12
Day 13	Day 14	Day 15	Day 16	Day 17	Day 18
Day 19	Day 20	Day 21	Day 22	Day 23	Day 24
Day 25	Day 26	Day 27	Day 28	Day 29	Day 30
Day 31					

Did you know that the moon travels around the Earth once every 29.7 days? It is commonly thought that the phases of the moon are caused by the shadow of the Earth falling on the moon, but this is not true! It is actually illuminated at different angles by the sun as it travels around the Earth.

Moon Phase Sandwich Cookies

Sandwich cookies (chocolate cookies with a layer of cream in between)

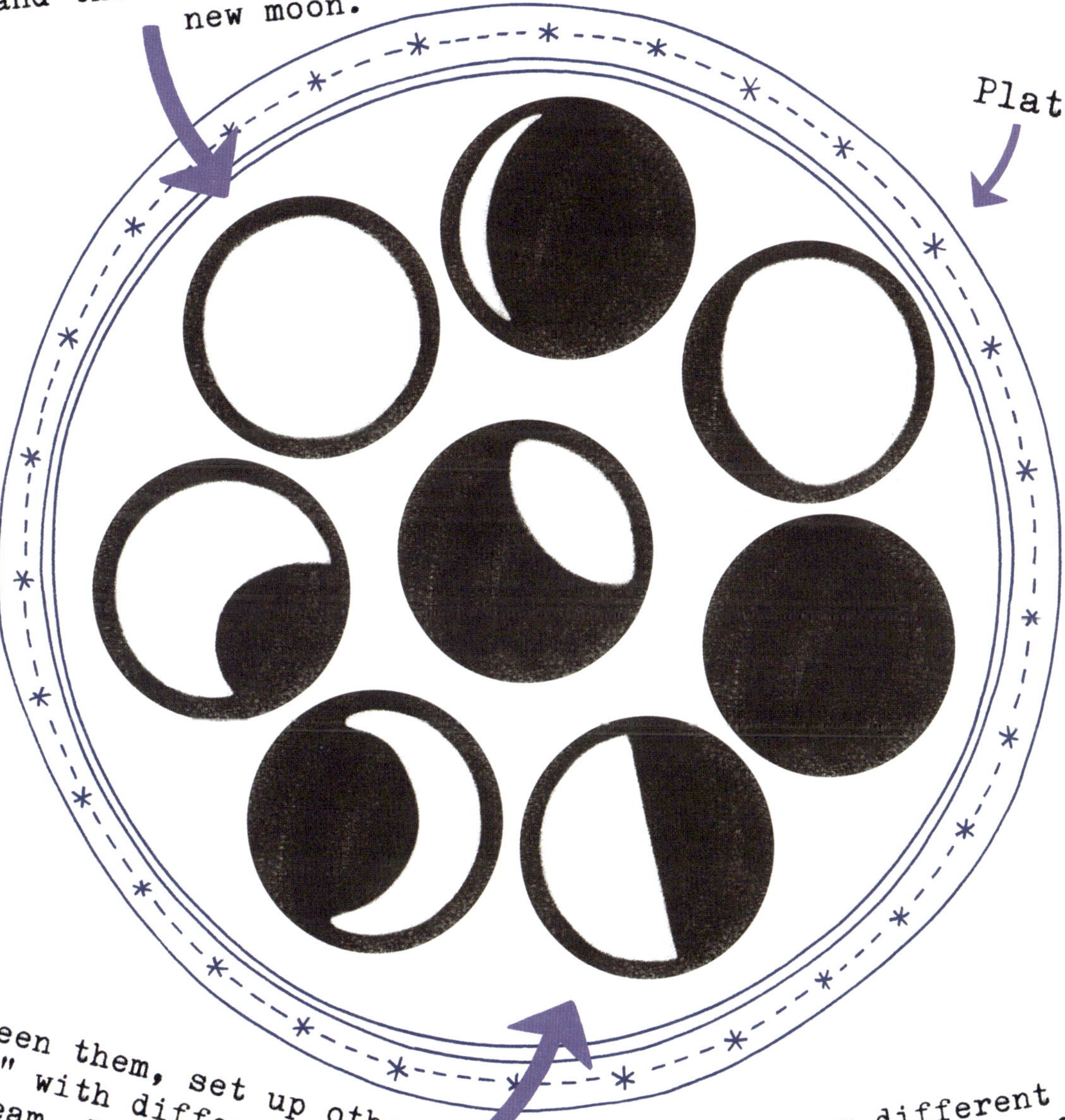

Take your first sandwich cookie and twist it apart so that the cream filling is completely on one side of the cookie. The other side should be as clean as possible. (Tip: Cut the cream with a butter knife and lift the excess away.) Place the cream-filling side on one end of your plate and the no-cream filling side on the other. The cream-filling side is a full moon, and the no-cream-filling side is a new moon.

Plate

Between them, set up other "moons" with different levels of cream. Try splitting the filling exactly in half for both of your half moons.

How many different phases can you make?

MOONMANIA

Earth is not the only planet with a moon. In fact, there are many moons in our solar system. Jupiter has an amazing 67 moons and Saturn has 62, many making up part of its rings.

Look in the puzzle below to discover some of the other moons you can find in our solar system! Look forwards, backwards, and diagonally.

Holiday on a MOON

Imagine you've gone to a moon!
Doodle where you would stay.

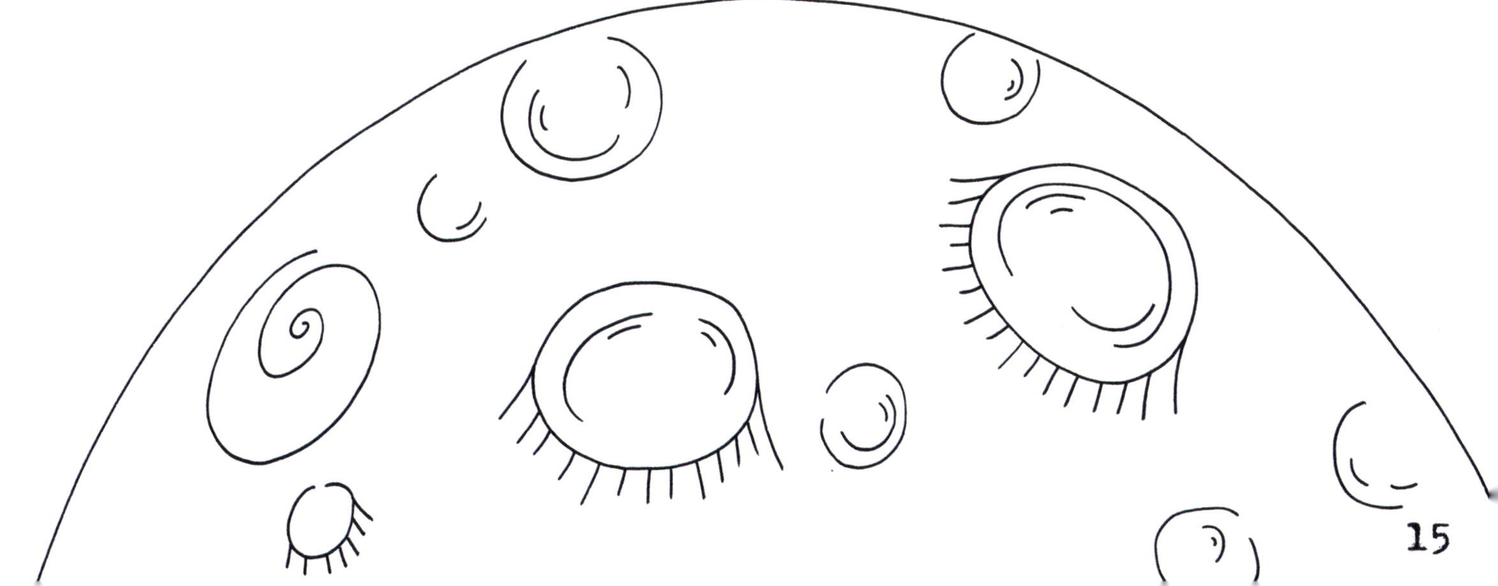

GOING ROVER

You're exploring Mars, the red planet! Guide the rover through the rocky Martian landscape to the giant crater at the end!

FINISH

Doodle what you think Martian life could look like!

DID YOU KNOW?

Mars once had oceans filled with water, much like ours, but its thinning atmosphere led to the planet losing most of its liquid water. Now almost all of the water on Mars is ice or vapor, but there is some evidence that liquid water still exists in very small quantities. Water on Mars might mean that life as we know it could exist there—our first inkling of life beyond Earth!

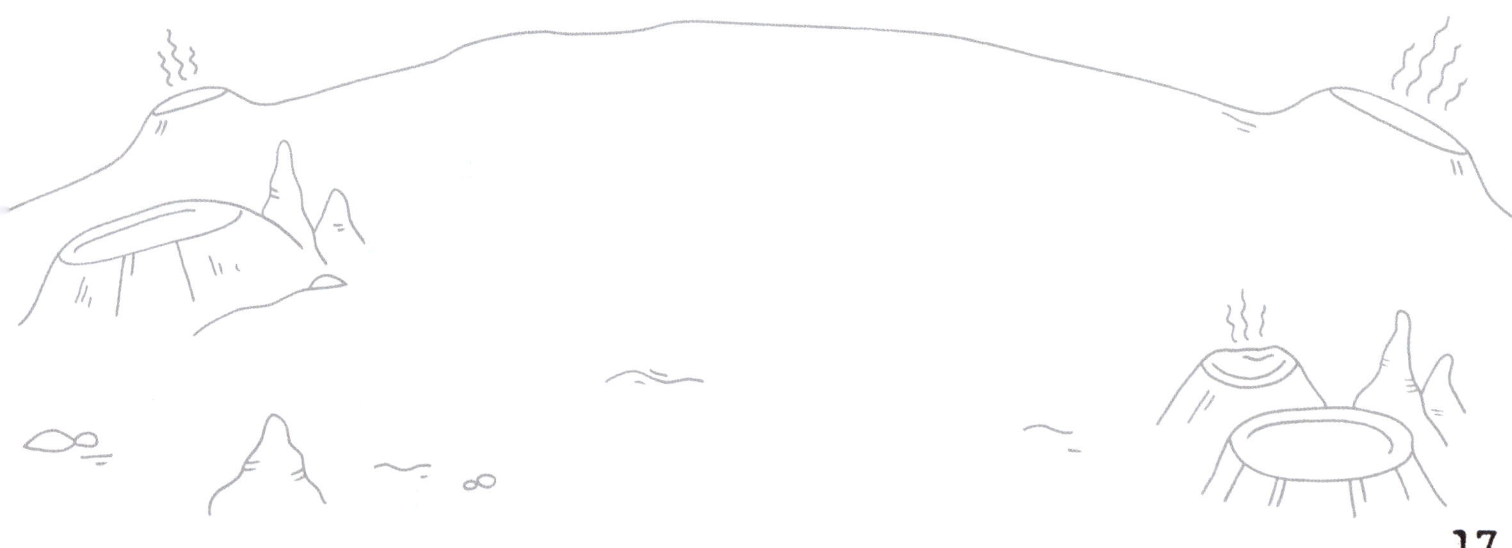

COMPLETE THE PLANETS

Jupiter is a gas giant, and the largest planet in our solar system.

Finish drawing patterns on Jupiter and the other planets, then color them in!

DID YOU KNOW?

Jupiter's most famous storm, the Great Red Spot, is so big it could fit three whole Earths inside it!

DID YOU KNOW?
A GAS GIANT is a massive planet that's made mostly of gases. The other gassy planets in our solar system are Saturn, Uranus, and Neptune. All the other planets—Mercury, Venus, Earth, and Mars—are called ROCKY PLANETS because they're made mostly of, you guessed it, rock!
How many stars can you count?

Fill in this spacey scene with planets, stars, black holes, asteroids, comets, and rockets!

DID YOU KNOW?

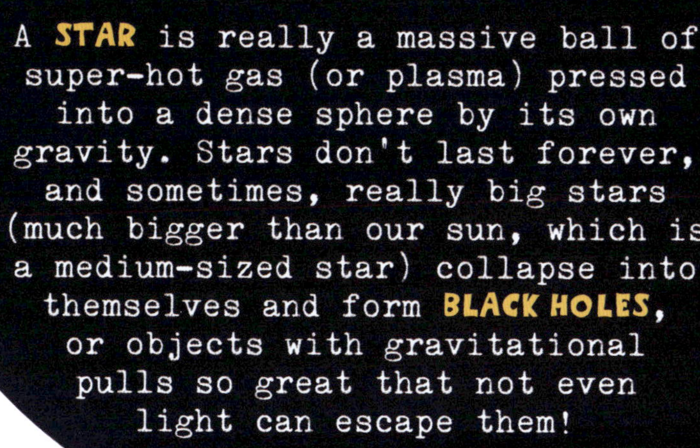

A **STAR** is really a massive ball of super-hot gas (or plasma) pressed into a dense sphere by its own gravity. Stars don't last forever, and sometimes, really big stars (much bigger than our sun, which is a medium-sized star) collapse into themselves and form **BLACK HOLES**, or objects with gravitational pulls so great that not even light can escape them!

OFF TO EXPLORE

C	D	H	L	M	R	X	T	C	G	B	L	A	N	D	E	R	U
O	O	Y	S	F	S	C	I	E	N	T	I	S	T	P	A	X	G
U	S	B	P	M	H	F	B	S	H	U	T	T	L	E	S	T	R
N	A	S	P	A	C	E	S	T	A	T	I	O	N	Q	T	E	A
T	T	M	O	O	N	L	A	N	D	I	N	G	D	J	R	L	V
D	E	K	D	O	C	K	I	N	G	K	K	B	Y	J	O	E	I
O	L	P	P	U	D	R	M	M	I	S	S	I	O	N	N	S	T
W	L	X	Q	H	V	S	P	A	C	E	W	A	L	K	A	C	Y
N	I	N	A	S	A	S	T	R	O	N	O	M	E	R	U	O	S
S	T	G	A	L	I	L	E	O	I	P	T	A	G	G	T	P	T
U	E	H	T	J	X	S	S	P	A	C	E	S	H	I	P	E	I
Q	U	A	P	O	L	L	O	L	A	U	N	C	H	V	M	Y	F

All of these words have to do with space exploration. Can you find them in the puzzle above? Look forwards, backwards, and up and down.

SHUTTLE
APOLLO
ASTRONOMER
SPACESHIP
ASTRONAUT
MISSION
MOON LANDING
COUNTDOWN
SPACE STATION
DOCKING
NASA
GALILEO
SPACEWALK
LANDER
SATELLITE
GRAVITY
LAUNCH
SCIENTIST
TELESCOPE

Draw yourself zooming off
into space and decorate
your rocket.
DID YOU KNOW?
APOLLO 11 was the name
of the mission that
first landed men on the
moon in 1969. The moon
is over 238,855 MILES
(384,340 km) away,
and it took them
4 days to get
there.

SPACE EXPLORER

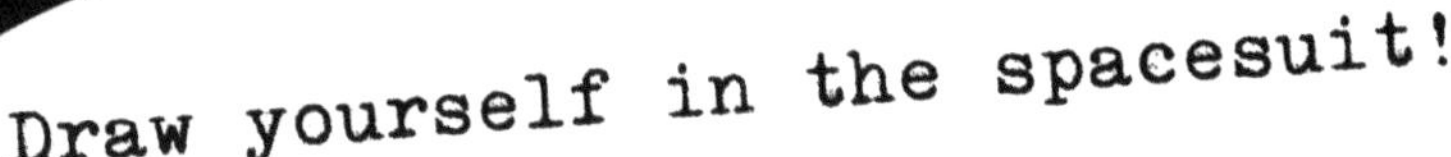

Draw yourself in the spacesuit!

Draw and color what you see as you explore space!

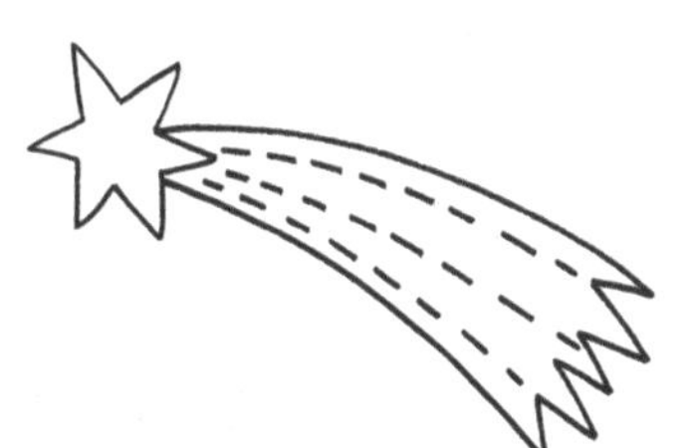

DID YOU KNOW?

An **ASTRONAUT** is someone who goes into space—a space explorer, if you will! **ROCKETS** are used to launch manned spacecraft, as well as satellites and probes. Sometimes, astronauts stay in space for months at a time within giant floating laboratories called **SPACE STATIONS**.

MONUMENTAL MISSIONS

Over the years humans have sent many spacecraft into orbit to explore other planets. Untangle the lines to see where each spacecraft went on its mission!

DID YOU KNOW?

Even though maps make our planetary neighbors look really close, they're actually super far away! For example, it took one of these spacecrafts 1,260 days to reach the closest planet to our sun, Mercury. That's almost four years!

Mercury
Jupiter
Saturn
Neptune
Uranus
Mars

Super Saturn

Saturn is famous for its rings—the discs made of ice, dust, and rock that surround it—but it's not the only planet that has them. Jupiter, Uranus, and Neptune all have faint rings of their own!

Give these planets rings, then add details and color them in!

Use the color key to reveal
this galactic scene!
1 2 3 4 5 6 7 8

You've made it to the asteroid belt between Mars and Jupiter! Draw yourself in the spaceship and fill the page with asteroids, then navigate your way through!

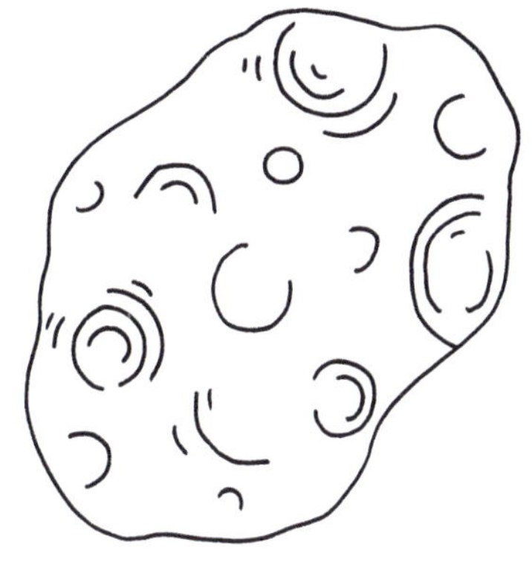

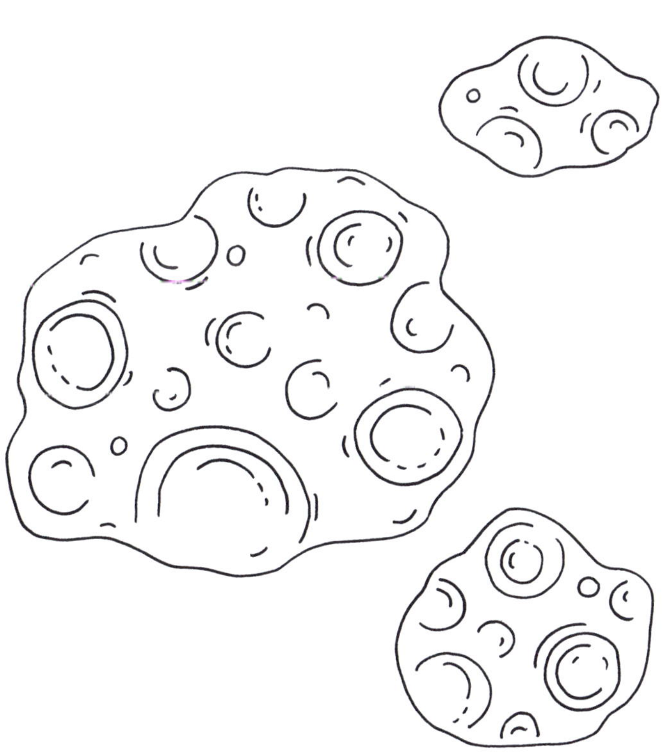

DID YOU KNOW?

COMETS are giant balls of ice, dust, and rock. The ice and dust melt together in sunlight and form a tail behind their comet. **ASTEROIDS** are giant balls of rock and metal that can be larger than a comet but do not have a tail.

MATCH THE METEOR
All of these meteors have a match. Can you find them all? Color each pair with matching colors!

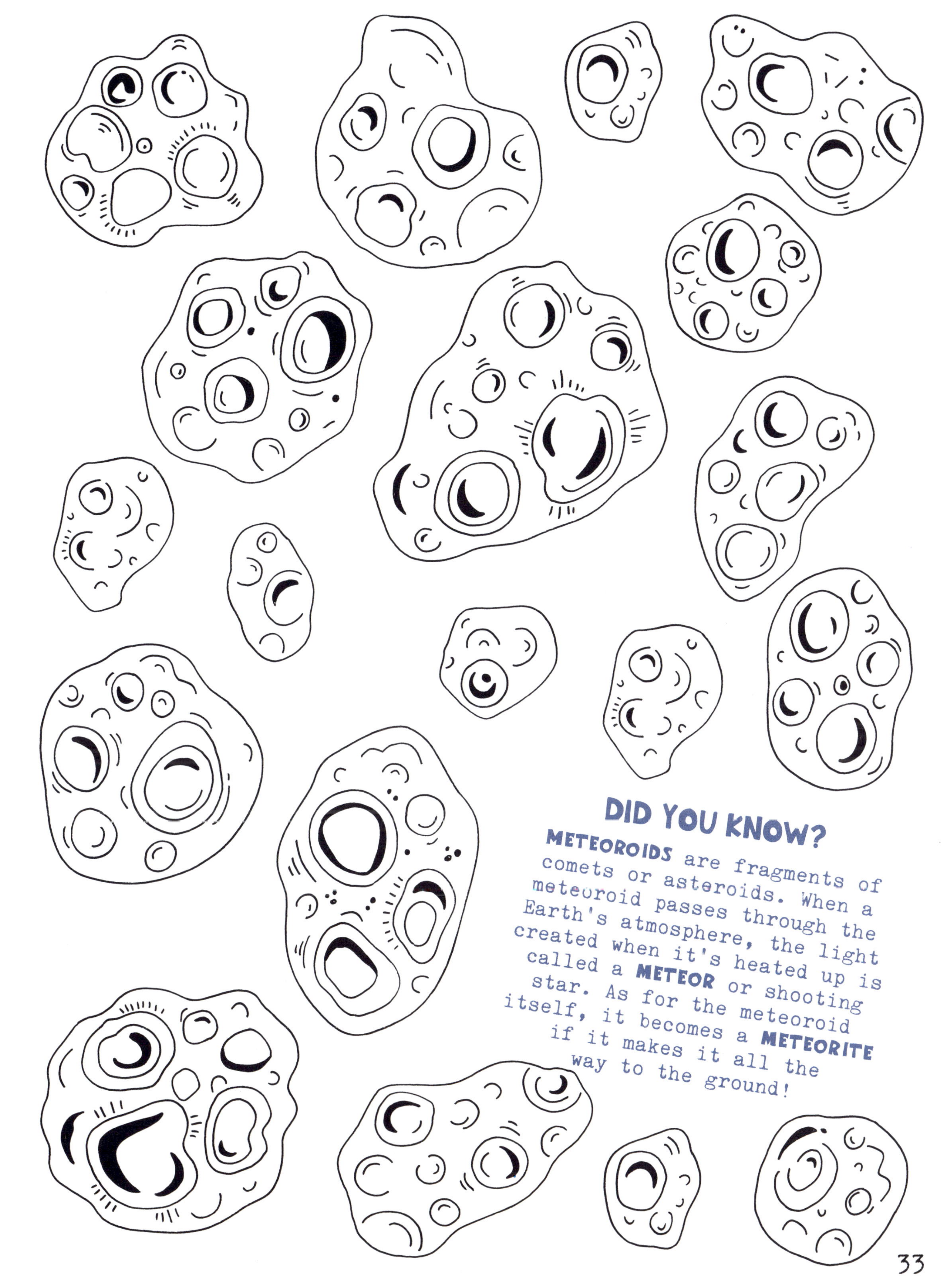
DID YOU KNOW?
METEOROIDS are fragments of comets or asteroids. When a meteoroid passes through the Earth's atmosphere, the light created when it's heated up is called a METEOR or shooting star. As for the meteoroid itself, it becomes a METEORITE if it makes it all the way to the ground!

MAKE A Sound Cone

You will need:

Poster board
Tape

1 Roll the poster board into a cone shape. Make sure one end is small enough to cup your ear, but make sure the other end is as big and wide as you can make it.

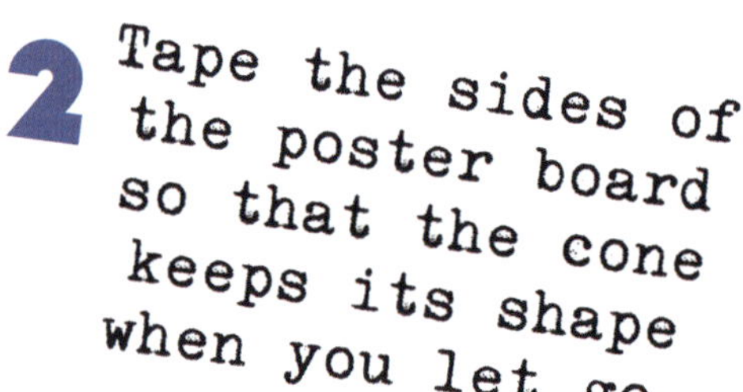

2 Tape the sides of the poster board so that the cone keeps its shape when you let go.

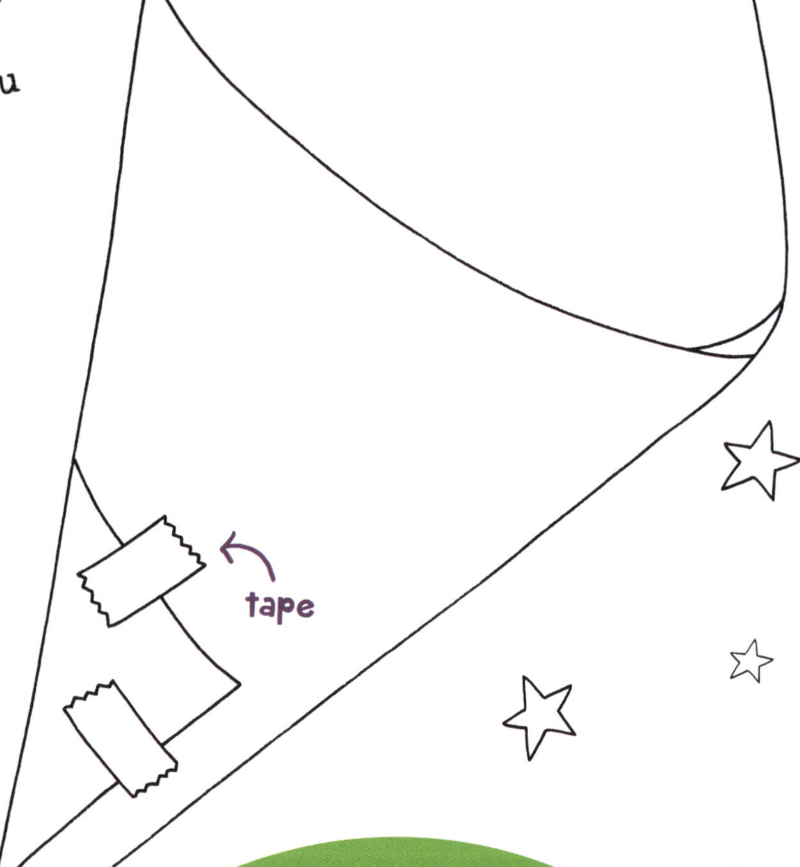

3 Go outside and put the smaller end of the cone up to your ear. What do you hear? This is how satellites and antennae collect information from space!

DID YOU KNOW?

Earth is currently the only known planet that hosts plant and animal life. However, since the 1960s, scientists have been searching for any sign of alien life, either by looking for planets that might support it or sending radio signals into outer space!

What would you send into space to show any potential aliens what it's like to live on Earth? Fill your space capsule!

SPACE CAPSULE

If you could speak to an alien, what would you say?

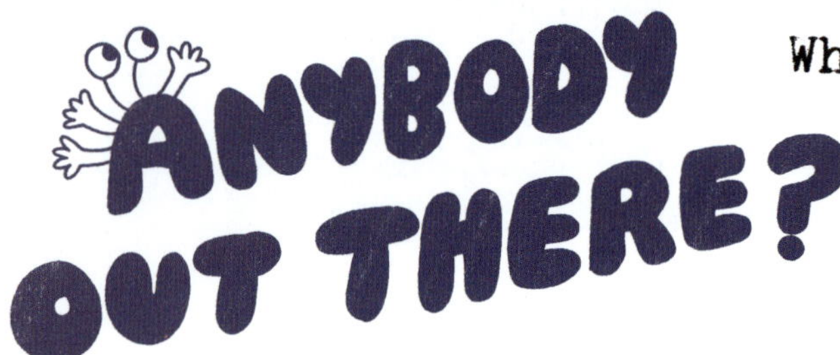

What do you think life on other planets could look like?

DESIGN YOUR OWN ALIEN

WHERE WOULD YOUR ALIEN LIVE?

Design a planet for it to live on!

What would you call your planet?

____

Can you spot the differences
between these 2 alien scenes?
There are 20 to find!

When you've found them all,
color in all the aliens
with two eyes!

CONSTELLATIONS

Connect the stars to reveal these famous constellations in the night sky.

Use the words at the bottom of each fact sheet to fill in the missing facts about each constellation.

10 9 11 8 6 12 7 Betelgeuse 5 4 3 2 1 16 13 17 14 15 Rigel

ORION

Orion is one of the most ________ constellations in the sky and can be seen throughout the ________. It contains two of the ________ stars in the sky, Rigel and ________. It was named after Orion, a ________ in Greek mythology.

WORLD **BETELGEUSE** **HUNTER** **BRIGHTEST** **RECOGNIZABLE**

DID YOU KNOW?

A **CONSTELLATION** is an area of the sky officially recognized by a group of astronomers known as the **INTERNATIONAL ASTRONOMICAL UNION.**

LEO

Named after the _____ in ________ mythology, Leo is home to ________, one of the brightest ________ in the night sky.

GREEK **STARS** **LION** **REGULUS**

2 1 3 11 4 10 5 9 6 Regulus 7 8

URSA MAJOR

Ursa _____ is the third largest _______________ in the sky and is also known as the Great _______. The body and tail are part of the Big _______________.

DIPPER MAJOR
BEAR CONSTELLATION

DID YOU KNOW?

An **ASTERISM** is a smaller grouping of stars, usually inside a constellation. The famous **BIG DIPPER** is an asterism that forms part of Ursa Major. Can you find it?

CARINA

Carina is found in the _____________ sky. Its name means the keel of a _______. The constellation is home to _________, the _________ brightest star in the sky.

SECOND SOUTHERN
CANOPUS SHIP

Canopus

In ancient times, astronomers saw images in different groups of stars. What can you see in the stars? Design your own constellation map!

On a piece of cardboard, trace over the stars in one of your constellations. With the help of an adult, use a sharp pencil to punch a hole through every star. (Tip: Place some cardboard behind your card, right behind each star, to avoid punching holes into anything else!) Wait until it is dark and then shine a light behind it to see your very own constellation!

DRAW A ROCKET

Follow the step-by-step instructions to draw your own rocket on the opposite page.

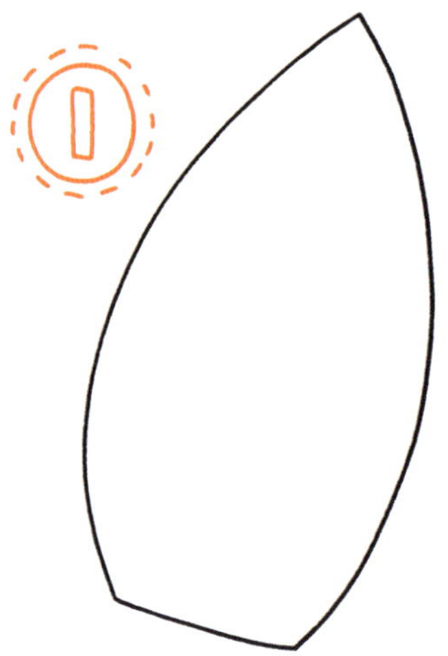

Start by drawing the body of the rocket.

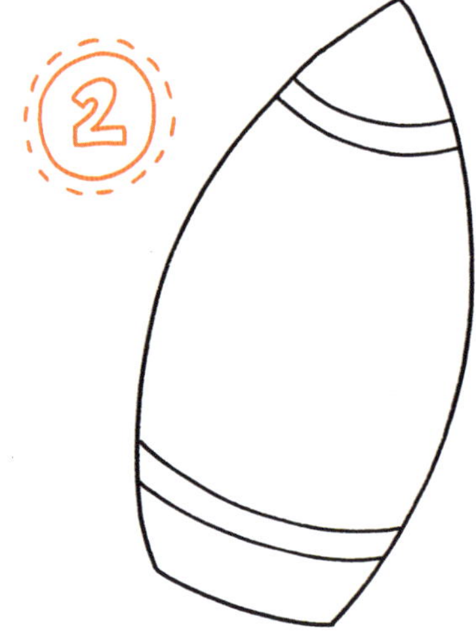

Add lines at the top and bottom of the rocket.

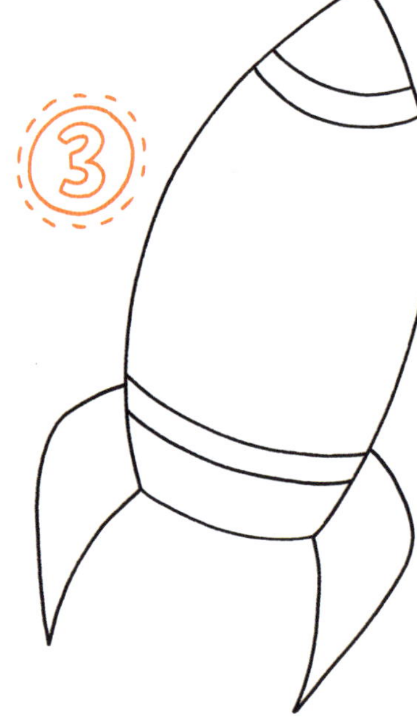

Add two boosters, one on each side.

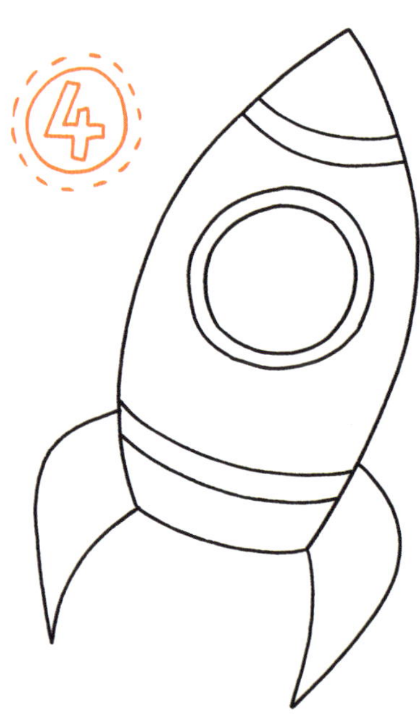

Draw a round window in the middle of the rocket.

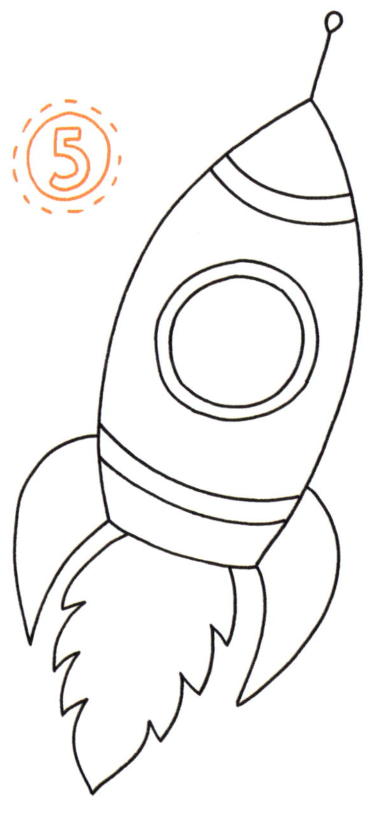

Add flames coming out of the bottom, and an antenna at the top.

Finish by adding stars and planets in the background.

NAME THE PLANET

As new planets are discovered, they need new names! What do you think would make a good name for a planet? Can you come up with a name for each letter of the alphabet?

A ____________ B ____________

C ____________ D ____________

E ____________ F ____________

G ____________ H ____________

I ____________ J ____________ K ____________

L ____________ M ____________

N ____________ O ____________

P ____________ Q ____________

R ____________ S ____________

T ____________ U ____________

V ____________ W ____________

X ____________ Y ____________

Z ____________

RICE PLANETS

YOU WILL NEED:

cooked rice (sushi rice works best!)

sheets of dried seaweed or nori (optional)

plastic wrap

FILLING

beans

cooked salmon

cheese

tuna

jelly

chicken nugget

1 Ask your parents to cook your rice until it's sticky. Wait until it's a little cool, then mix in a few drops of food coloring until all your rice has been dyed.

You can separate rice into different bowls and color each with a different dye, if you want multicolored planets!

2 When the rice is cool enough to touch, spread your plastic wrap over one hand and scoop enough rice to cover your palm. Make a little dent in the center and add a little bit of filling for the planet's core.

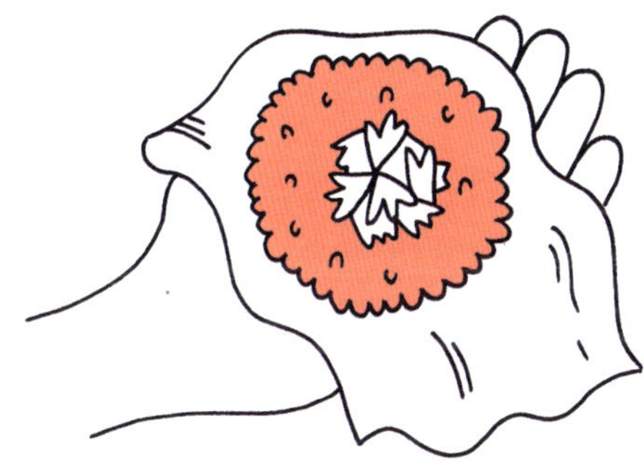

3 Pull the edges of the plastic wrap together so that the rice makes a ball inside. Be sure to keep the filling on the inside of your planet! Twist the edges of the plastic wrap together and gently squeeze the rice with one hand until it forms a perfect sphere.

4 Unwrap the first rice planet and repeat the steps to make the next. If you'd like, cut "continents" out of dried seaweed, moisten one side with water, and press it onto the side of your rice planet.

LIFE IN SPACE

Imagine life on the International Space Station. What would you do in zero gravity?

What would it look like if you lived there? Draw yourself and your rooms in it!

DID YOU KNOW?

The International Space Station is a giant laboratory orbiting Earth. Up to six people can live in it full-time, and it's used by scientists from all over the world to study everything from human biology to astrophysics. The research conducted there will one day help us determine whether or not humans can colonize other planets or go on long space flights.

SOLAR SYSTEM MAZE

Navigate your way through the planets and comets in our solar system to get to the sun at the center!

DID YOU KNOW?

The sun is so far away that it takes 8 minutes and 20 seconds for its light to reach Earth!

ORIGAMI SHUTTLE

You will need one piece of rectangular colored paper.

1

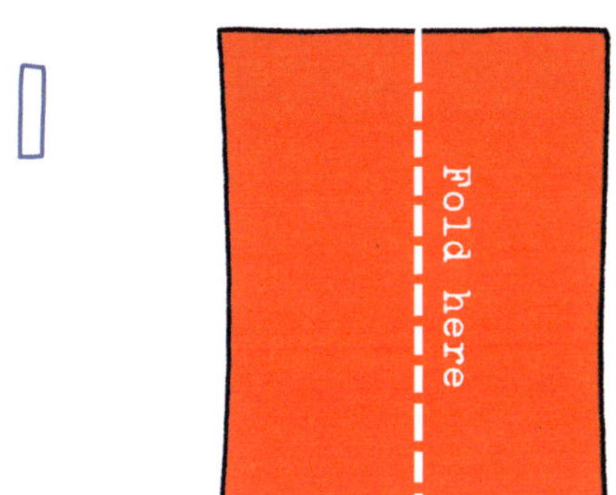

Fold the paper in half, then unfold.

2

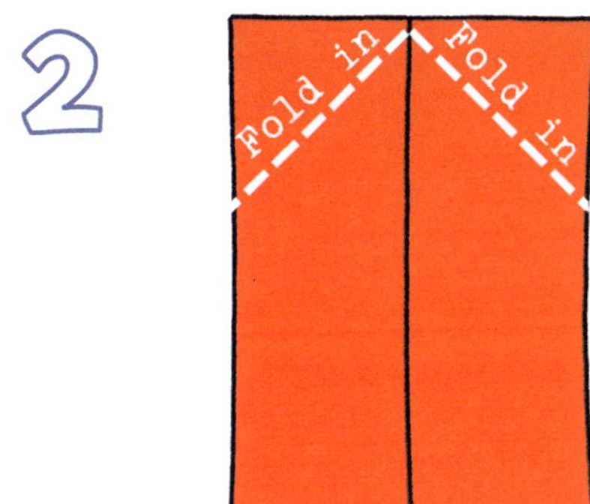

Fold the top two corners in toward the center line.

3

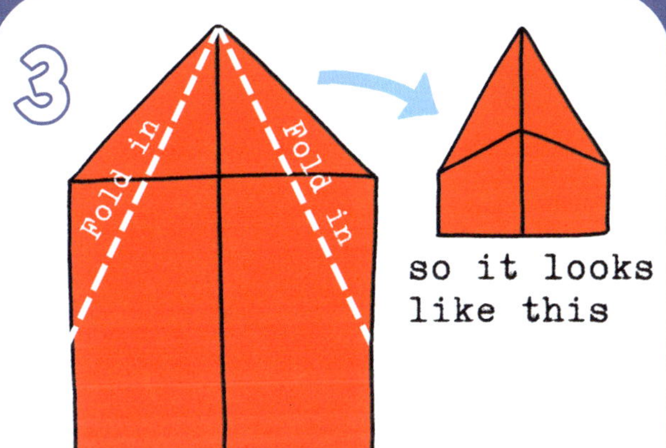

so it looks like this

Fold the left and right sides inwards to the center line.

4

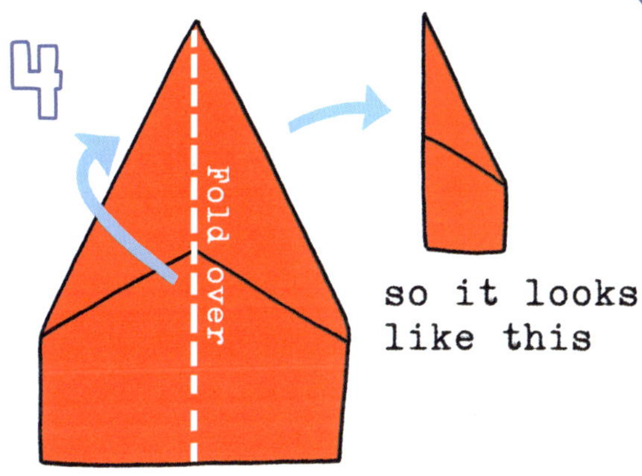

so it looks like this

Fold over in half.

5

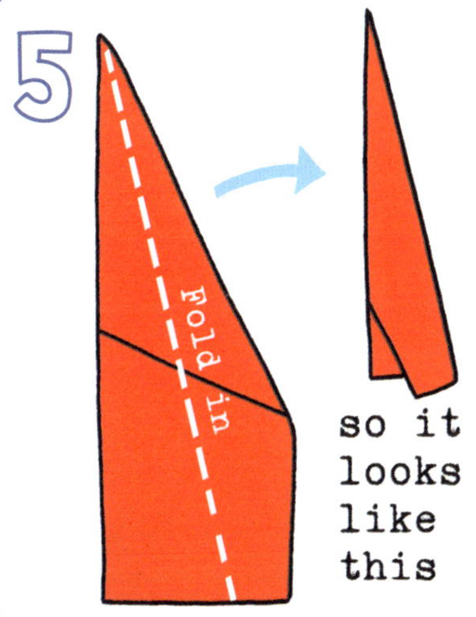

so it looks like this

Taking one side of the the shuttle, fold the outer edge inwards. Turn the shuttle over and repeat on the other side. Now that your shuttle is complete, test its flying skills!

NASA's space shuttle took off like a rocket and glided back to Earth's surface like a plane.

GALAXIES

A galaxy is a massive group of billions of stars and other objects, all orbiting around a central point. Sometimes, these galaxies are shaped like giant spirals with arms stretching out in all directions. Our galaxy is known as the Milky Way, and our solar system is smack in the middle of one of its numerous arms!

DID YOU KNOW?

The closest galaxy to us is the Andromeda Galaxy. It is also a spiral galaxy like the Milky Way. Although it is the closest to us, it is still a whopping 2.5 million light years away! On a clear night it can be spotted with the naked eye.

Color this swirling galaxy in pinks, purples, blues, reds, and oranges!

GALACTIC UNIVERSE

The universe is made up of billions and billions of galaxies, all full of stars, planets, and other objects! Use these central points to fill the page with galaxies. Some could be disc-shaped and some could have spiral arms like the Milky Way. Once you're done, color them in!

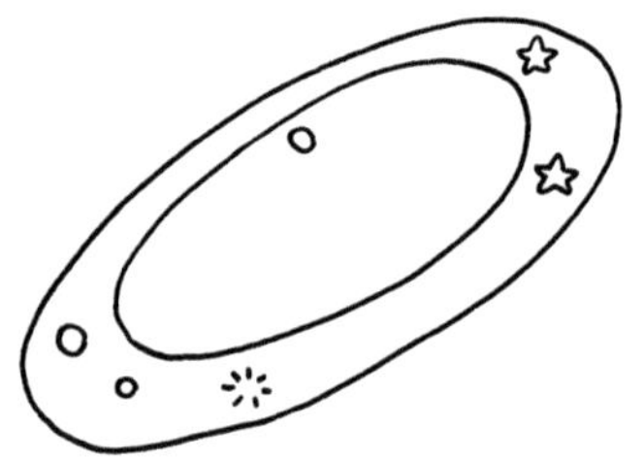

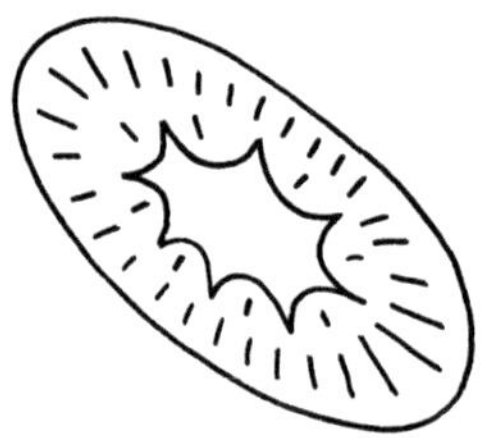

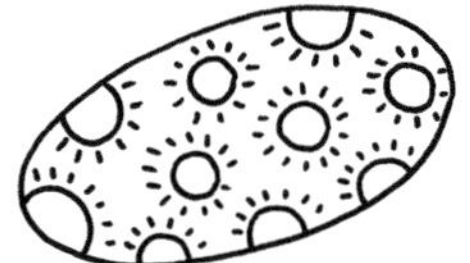

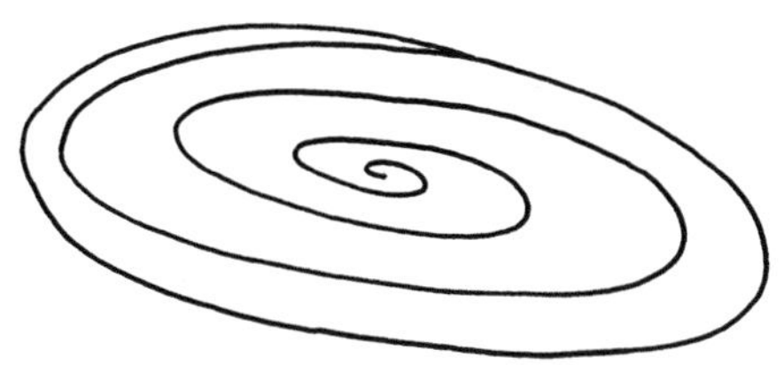

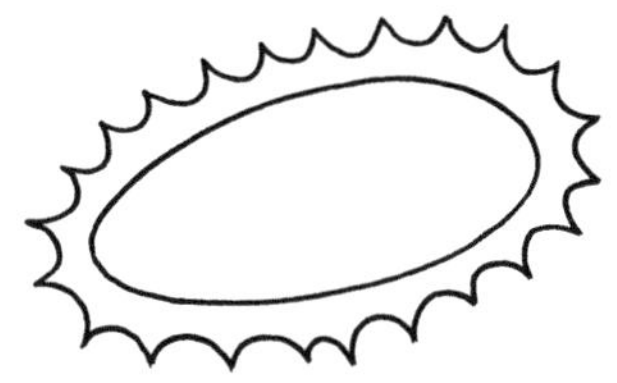

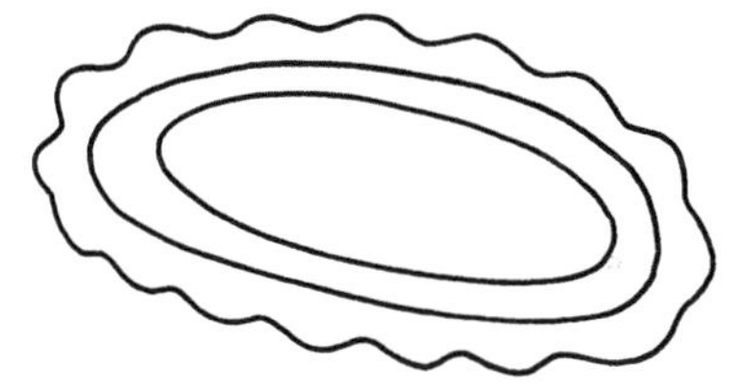

How many of these space objects can you find?
Color as you go to keep count!
satellites
meteor showers
galaxies
planets with rings
planets
black holes
rockets
asteroids
meteors
moons
quasars
comets
stars
dwarf planets

DID YOU KNOW?

A **DWARF** or **MINOR PLANET** is an object that looks and orbits the sun like a planet, but it's much smaller than one. Pluto, which was once our smallest planet, is now called a dwarf planet. **QUASARS** are giant objects that give off more light and energy than anything else in a galaxy. At the center of each quasar is a supermassive black hole!

ACROSS

3. This planet is named after the Roman goddess of love and beauty
4. No longer classed as a planet because it is too small
5. Some planets are made of rock, while others are made of _ _ _
8. Giant ball of rock and metal zooming through space!
9. Dark patch of space with a huge gravitational pull
11. Giant balls of gas that light up the universe
13. Closest planet to the sun, and as a result the hottest
15. Astronauts live here for months at a time
17. The name of our galaxy and a tasty chocolate!
19. The star Earth orbits around
20. Massive group of billions of stars and other objects
21. Giant ball of ice and dust, known for having a tail

DOWN

1. Scientists believe the _ _ _ _ _ _ _ _ was created as a result of the Big Bang
2. The largest planet orbiting our sun
6. The group of planets and star that the Earth is part of
7. A natural satellite
8. Someone who goes into space
10. The path of a planet around a star
12. Vehicle that launches into space
14. Some planets have these, and people wear them on their fingers
16. Planet famous for its discs of ice, dust, and rock
18. The red planet

1

ASTRONAUTS and **ASTRONOMERS** need very good math and logic skills to help make new discoveries and calculate complex equations!

Test out your logic skills with these **SUDOKU** puzzles!

EACH ROW, COLUMN, AND BOX IN THE GRID MUST CONTAIN THE NUMBERS 1-4 ONLY ONCE.

Can you work out where the remaining numbers should go?

2

	1		
4	3	1	
1			4

3

4

SOLAR SHIFTING

Many cultures used the movement of the sun, moon, and stars to keep track of time. This is possible because our planet rotates at an even speed, so the sun, moon, and stars seem to move across the sky at a steady pace throughout the day and night—even though we're the ones who are moving! You can make your own solar clock (or sundial) just like ancient astronomers by following the steps below.

1. Grab this book, a small object, and a flashlight.

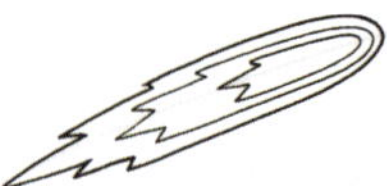

2. Stand your object up on top of the sun in the center of this page. This activity works best if your object isn't too big so its shadow doesn't stray too far from the edge of this book.

3. Move the flashlight in an arc over this book, just like the sun "moves" in an arc across the sky. Try to go at a steady pace, without speeding up or slowing down. What do you notice about your object's shadow as you move?

FOR A FUN TWIST,

try it outside! Wait for a sunny day, then line up your book with a spot you'll remember later (such as a crack in the sidewalk or the edge of a table). Place your object on this page, and use a piece of chalk, a stick, or whatever else you can find to trace the shadow it casts. Then come back in ten minutes and do it again!

Or for a you-shaped sundial, draw an X on the sidewalk or ground and stand on top of it, then have a friend trace your shadow. Because you're bigger than the object you used above be sure to wait a half an hour or more before adding to your sundial.

MILKY WAY MODEL

Make your own model of the Milky Way! When you're finished, ask an adult to hang it up for you.

You will need:

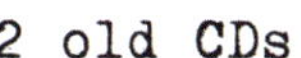
2 old CDs

1 piece of paper

Permanent marker

an adult assistant

Crumple the piece of paper into a ball, making it as round as you can.

2 Glue the CDs together shiny side out. You may need hot glue instead of ordinary paper glue, at which point your adult assistant should be able to help you.

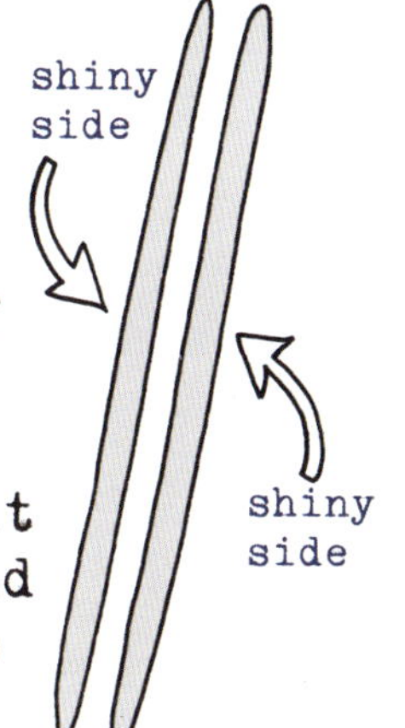

3

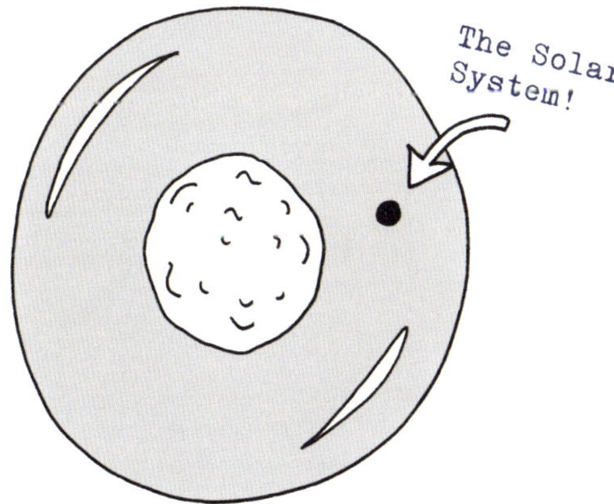

Push the ball of paper into the hole in the CDs so that half sticks out of the other side. Make a dot halfway out from the center of your galaxy. This is roughly where our solar system is in the Milky Way!

4

Look at the disc from the side, lining up your eyes with the dot you've made. Notice how everything looks flat, except for the big, bulky ball in the center? This is why the Milky Way looks like a narrow band in the night sky, even though it's actually much, much bigger than that!

ANSWERS

Pages 6-7

SOLAR SCRAMBLE

A group of objects (planets, comets, asteroids, and more) that move around a star is called a solar system. Our solar system contains eight planets and one star, plus countless smaller objects! Unscramble the letters below to discover the biggest objects in our solar system!

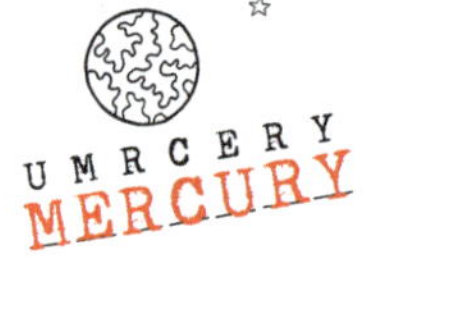

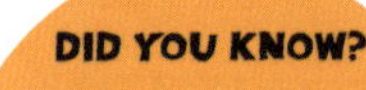

- U M R C E R Y – MERCURY
- E P N U T N E – NEPTUNE
- A E R H T – EARTH
- S T A R N U – SATURN
- U N S – SUN
- S A R M – MARS
- P I J U T R E – JUPITER
- S U N V E – VENUS
- U S A U R N – URANUS

DID YOU KNOW?

Except for Earth, all of the planets in our solar system are named after Roman gods and goddesses. For example, the second planet from the sun, Venus, was named after the Roman goddess of love and beauty!

Page 14

MOONMANIA

D	E	I	M	O	S	S	B	S	S	E	F	J	O	R
I	K	J	S	L	U	T	E	I	U	U	C	T	T	N
V	K	L	E	E	R	D	A	R	D	R	B	W	X	D
F	Y	I	T	I	E	P	I	Z	A	O	K	I	O	A
I	R	O	T	M	E	Q	C	H	L	P	N	E	J	I
A	R	O	Y	T	S	O	H	R	E	A	G	X	A	N
P	N	N	U	L	X	C	K	J	C	Z	W	H	M	A
C	A	S	G	U	E	D	Y	S	N	O	M	I	A	T
G	A	D	N	A	R	I	M	P	E	G	A	Y	L	I
O	O	L	R	H	E	A	R	A	H	I	M	L	T	T
N	X	E	L	Q	O	V	K	B	N	O	A	I	H	C
Z	M	N	D	I	E	R	E	N	M	T	B	K	E	R
F	A	O	E	G	S	Z	P	G	G	U	I	O	A	U
F	O	I	S	E	S	T	G	L	S	C	K	T	S	H
T	U	D	F	O	X	P	O	L	F	J	I	Z	N	W

Page 16

GOING ROVER

ANSWERS

Pages 18-19

Number of stars: **42**

Page 22

OFF TO EXPLORE

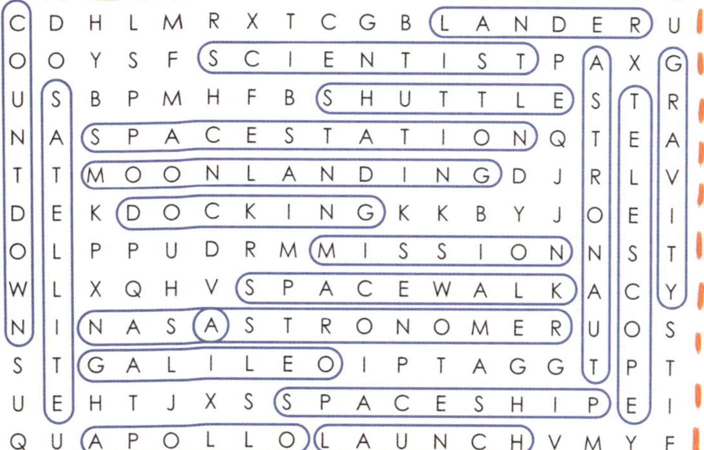

Pages 26-27
Monumental Missions

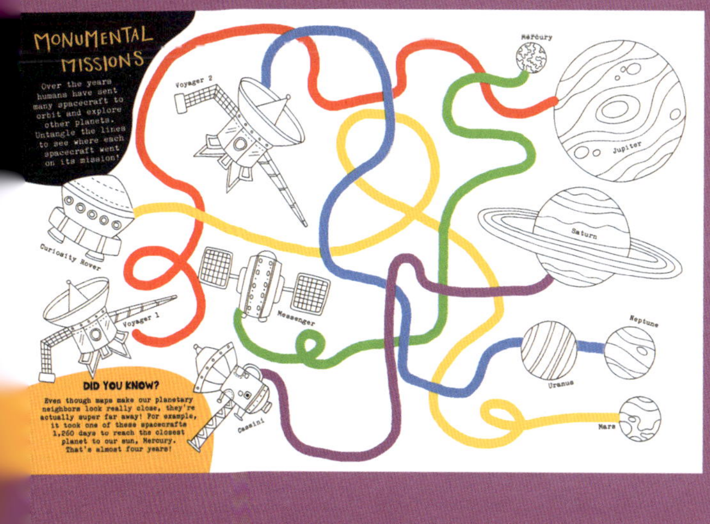

Pages 32-33
Matching pairs

Pages 38-39
Spot the Difference

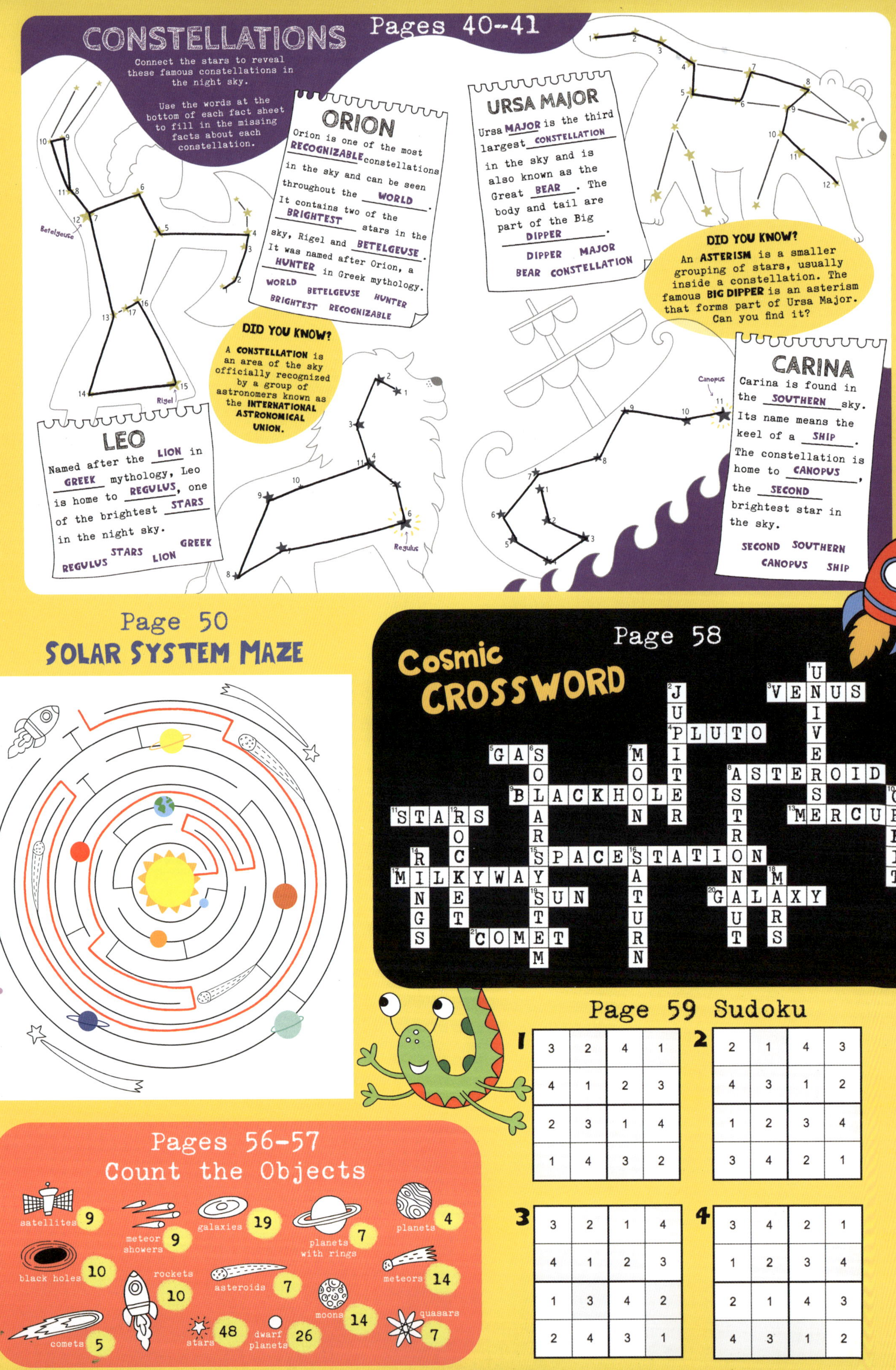

CONSTELLATIONS
Pages 40–41
Connect the stars to reveal these famous constellations in the night sky.
Use the words at the bottom of each fact sheet to fill in the missing facts about each constellation.
Betelgeuse
Rigel
ORION
Orion is one of the most RECOGNIZABLE constellations in the sky and can be seen throughout the WORLD. It contains two of the brightest BRIGHTEST stars in the sky, Rigel and BETELGEUSE. It was named after Orion, a HUNTER in Greek mythology.
WORLD BETELGEUSE HUNTER BRIGHTEST RECOGNIZABLE
URSA MAJOR
Ursa MAJOR is the third largest CONSTELLATION in the sky and is also known as the Great BEAR. The body and tail are part of the Big DIPPER.
DIPPER MAJOR BEAR CONSTELLATION
DID YOU KNOW?
An ASTERISM is a smaller grouping of stars, usually inside a constellation. The famous BIG DIPPER is an asterism that forms part of Ursa Major. Can you find it?
DID YOU KNOW?
A CONSTELLATION is an area of the sky officially recognized by a group of astronomers known as the INTERNATIONAL ASTRONOMICAL UNION.
LEO
Named after the LION in GREEK mythology, Leo is home to REGULUS, one of the brightest STARS in the night sky.
REGULUS STARS LION GREEK
Regulus
Canopus
CARINA
Carina is found in the SOUTHERN sky. Its name means the keel of a SHIP. The constellation is home to CANOPUS, the SECOND brightest star in the sky.
SECOND SOUTHERN CANOPUS SHIP
Page 50
SOLAR SYSTEM MAZE
Page 58
Cosmic CROSSWORD
1 UNIVERSE, 2 JUPITER, 3 VENUS, 4 PLUTO, 5 GAS, 6 SOLAR SYSTEM, 7 MOON, 8 ASTEROID, 8 ASTRONAUT, 9 BLACK HOLE, 10 ORBIT, 11 STARS, 12 ROCKET, 13 MERCURY, 14 RINGS, 15 SPACE STATION, 16 SATURN, 17 MILKY WAY, 18 MARS, 19 SUN, 20 GALAXY, 21 COMET
Page 59 Sudoku
1
3 2 4 1
4 1 2 3
2 3 1 4
1 4 3 2
2
2 1 4 3
4 3 1 2
1 2 3 4
3 4 2 1
3
3 2 1 4
4 1 2 3
1 3 4 2
2 4 3 1
4
3 4 2 1
1 2 3 4
2 1 4 3
4 3 1 2
Pages 56–57
Count the Objects
satellites 9
meteor showers 9
galaxies 19
planets with rings 7
planets 4
black holes 10
rockets 10
asteroids 7
meteors 14
moons 14
quasars 7
comets 5
stars 48
dwarf planets 26